Copyright © 2020 Ana M. Jinga All rights reserved

The characters and events portrayed in this book are fictitious. Any similarity to real persons, living or dead, is coincidental and not intended by the author.

No part of this book may be reproduced, or stored in a retrieval system, or transmitted in any form or by any means, electronic, mechanical, photocopying, recording, or otherwise, without express written permission of the publisher.

ISBN paperback: 9798666256381

Cover design by: Kindle Cover Design

Imprint: Independently Printed

For the dreamer inside your heart.
Thank you for believing in me & being by my side through all the ups & downs.

With so much love,
Ana J.

TRUTH
LEFT
UNSPOKEN

CONTENTS

TRUTH LEFT UNSPOKEN

1 Collections of Love

2 About Chaos & Pain

3 Magical Healing

I dedicate this book to love.

The beauty of love for another,
The healing of love for one's self.

Honoring each of these two will bring forth the truth that will help you on your path through Life.

When is the
last time
you took
a deep breath?

Take one now.

My dear readers,

I first want to thank you for being here, for holding space for these words and thoughts to flow. I am so grateful for you!

Secondly, please be advised that some of the poems might be triggering. If that happens come back to this page and follow the next steps:

Take a deep breath in.

Hold it for a count of 3 slow seconds.

Open up your mouth and let it ALL out: either sigh it out, scream it out or cry it out.

The feeling you are now experiencing is part of your healing. Come back to a slow steady breath.

Observe what comes up.

Notice any thoughts as mere clouds on a perfectly blue sky. Know that these clouds, regardless of how dark they are, they're just passing by.

These thoughts are no longer your reality. They are memories which have built you up into the beautiful strong human being that you are at this very moment.

Place a hand on your heart and one on your belly. Allow yourself to witness your breath how comfortably easy it flows.

Bring a sense of gratitude for your breath.

And know, my dear reader, that as you are, right now at this very moment, you are MORE THAN ENOUGH.

Take another deep breath in and let it out.

Thank you again for being here and reading my thoughts and rhymes.

I wish you many blessings and love.

With kindness and compassion,

Anthem

We rise
Step by step.
We rise
From the depths.
We rise
Like the waves.
We rise
On the crests.
We rise
From the blood.
We rise
From our deaths.

Confessions of Love

*You held a safe space for me
to come back to myself
without telling me what to do
or how to do it.
You just knew I would know
on my own.*

*Your embrace silenced
the darkest demons
inside my mind.*

*Seeing you smile always
made me happy
even if
it wasn't because
of me.*

*We never needed
words.
The energy was enough
to say it all.*

*Stay still and hold me tighter.
Hold me longer
until I don't know where
my skin ends
and yours begins.*

*Even though you weren't looking
when you found him,
it was him you needed most
and fought so hard not to want him,
but when there are matters of love at play,
the needing and the wanting
become
the same exact thing.*

*I drew my fingers
on your lips
and they became
mine.*

*I've opened up my heart
to people
and they mocked me.
Now all I want to do
is open up my heart to you,
but I'm afraid.*

*My cup could never run dry
when pouring onto you.
The more I pour
the more you fill me up.*

*One time you held my hand.
It felt so natural
I couldn't understand
how it all felt
so familiar
and you just surrendered
to my touch
knowing you were
always safe.*

*I didn't choose you.
The whole Universe
decided it was you.*

Your demons never scared me.
No matter how many layers
of your past and pain
you would unravel
it never fazed me.
I've walked through hell before
Many times meeting
All that darkness.

Your scent follows me.
Kind of haunting.
Kind of familiar.
Like from another time.
Like from another lifetime.

*You and I.
We shared so much
and it all started with
the same sky.
With the same mystical Moon
And all those hypnotic Stars.*

*So easily,
You saw right through me,
through all the layers.
But what surprised you was that
so did I.*

*I'll share my dreams,
you share your scars.
We'll learn together
how to blend them.*

*Give me your Forever
and I will never put it down.
I shall Cherish it,
Care for it,
Nurture it,
Vow it my Forever.*

*I had a dream
One night among all my
prophetic glimpses of life.
You read my words,
You read right through.
Suddenly you flipped a coin
To see if you too
Could confess your love,
But then I just awoke..
You still haven't told me
How you really feel.*

*I'm never truly lost.
When I miss you most
I just close my eyes and see you,
smiling back at me.*

It's you.
It's been you
all this time.
A hundred thousand lifetimes
and it's still you.

*The softness of your hands
and vastness of your heart
have opened my soul
to awaken.*

*I wished for years to be
Invisible.
To blend in and hide from sight.
But one day you showed up
and all I wanted was
just for You
to see me.*

*The depth of your gaze
Struck so deeply,
But behind it there's an ocean of
knowledge and experience,
a sea of memories and walls,
a consciousness so rich
it could trap me for ages without escape.
I could always tell how tired your soul was
By how your eyes just got lost sometimes.*

*The lingering thoughts
Of all the you's and them's
Out there
That once were sharing air
With me
Simply faded
When my eyes met yours.
Those beautiful warm eyes
That made love to my soul
The very first second they met.*

*They say you can't actually heal or fix
someone.
When, in fact, you can.
You can heal them with your presence,
with your love,
the way you hold space,
the way you share your energy and
nurturing wits with them.
You heal them by being who you
were meant to be.
You can't heal them by doing something in
particular,
but just by being who
you truly are.*

What did it take
for you to feel
all that pain
so deeply and still
hold onto it like
it was your air?

*About
Chaos & Pain*

*Once the darkness sets,
the demons come out,
each one crawling its way
into my mind.*

*Your flowers are just simple drops of ice
in a river of burning lava.
They won't fix the ravaging flames
you created inside me.*

*Broken isn't a trend.
It's a lifelong reality.
Some of us
held our broken pieces
in our bloody hands
for what felt like eons at a time
without even knowing how
we could ever put them
back together.*

*Tears of blood
and death of soul
is what a love war
feels like.*

*They broke you, yes.
But you refused
to put yourself back.
You wore it like a trophy
like a Martyr,
not noticing how much it was tearing
at your Soul.
How much it was changing
your whole damn structure.*

*My scars don't show
on the inside.
The rivers of pain
flowing so effortlessly
through my body
are invisible to
the untrained eye.*

*For a moment there
I forgot
I was still
breathing.*

*The only thing holding me,
In that moment,
was the cold wet
bathroom floor.
It felt comforting.
It felt safe to crash and break into
a hundred thousand tiny glass pieces
that once formed my fragile heart.*

*You broke me from
the inside out,
yet expected me
to still be fine.
To look fine,
to sound Fine.
So I learned to numb it all,
no feelings to show,
no depth to surface,
just a simple lifeless mask
to numb it all.*

All that shaking,
Trembling,
Shivering is from
the earthquake
of all my broken pieces
crumbling down.
The foundation I once
Built myself on
Was viciously being shattered away...

*I cringe
at the thought
of you once telling me
'I love you'.*

*Shallow is the name
that caused
my inner child
to bleed.*

*I had to break myself
to pieces
to push through
all that numbness.*

*My chest was torn
To all four corners
By a single word
Yet smiling is what I do best
When I hurt.*

*When Angels cried
with tears of blood.
the numbness reigned
under the broken pieces
of what was once
a girl.*

*The pain you caused
Felt like a punishment
I deserved.
I didn't know better.*

*I was never taught
To love myself.
Only to sacrifice myself.
And that,
I learned later in life,
would cost me
my safety.*

*I chant…
And curse…
I scream…
And cry…
To heal two dozen years.
Yet, they expect me
to be okay
in a day.*

*I looked for comfort
in all the men
I ever met.
Yet, all I really needed
was a Father.*

The Devil is in the details.
Like how you gave me a nice word
or a comforting smile
just to make me feel like
I'm crazy for believing
you could be
harmful for me.

*The Pain
was tearing me up inside,
so I numbed it under
a shaking smile.*

Numb,
I breathe slow and shallow.
Numb,
I freeze when you speak.
Numb,
The feelings are painful.
Numb,
The strike was too much.
Numb.
My mind slowly fades in darkness.
Numb,
I began to shiver in tears.
Numb,
A part of me died that day.

*Pain is pain,
No matter how it was felt.
There is no lesser or greater form of it,
pain will always
crack you open
from the inside out.
It will shred you
so violently open
that you won't know how
to cover yourself back up.*

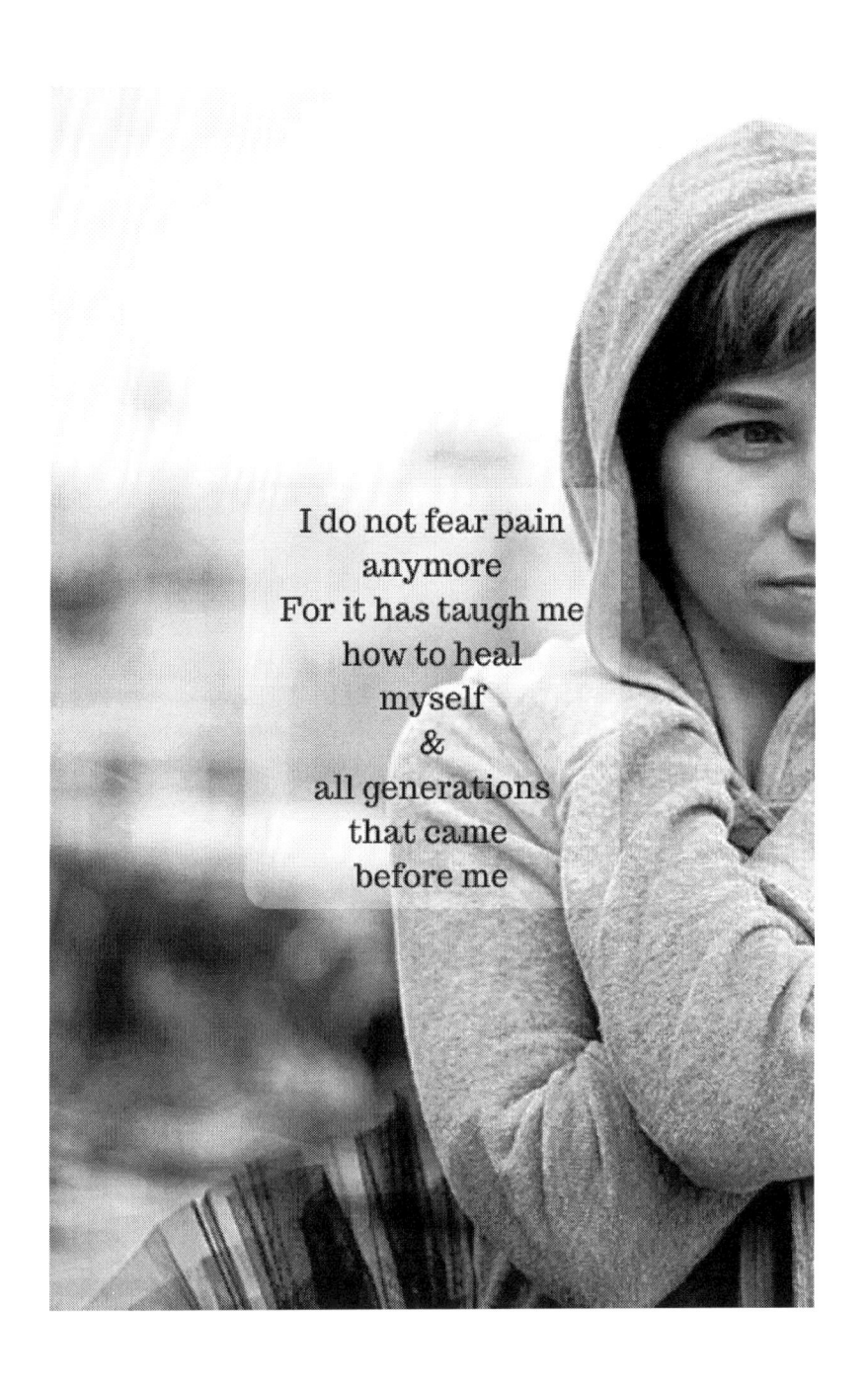

I do not fear pain
anymore
For it has taugh me
how to heal
myself
&
all generations
that came
before me

Magical Healing

*The heart can break
a thousand times,
yet you'll still be
Alive.*

*The lies are much
too much to handle;
I'm building
my own truth.*

*Being a woman doesn't make me weak.
Being a man doesn't make you entitled
To make me feel weak.*

*Heal yourself from
the inside out,
not the other way
around.
It always starts with you.
Just you.*

*Shards are falling
behind me
once I decide
it's time to
walk away.*

*Lost is not a chapter,
it's where you go to find
a glimpse of yourself.
To rediscover who you were
Before all this occurred.
Before they hurt you
Into believing
You were not enough.*

*Of course it was
All in my own mind.
That's what was actually sick
inside of me.*

*The hands that grabbed me,
or the lips that viciously tore
at my soul
never truly claimed me.
I first belong to ME.*

*My body's shape,
size,
weight,
form,
complexion
or texture,
do not
concern you.
They never did.*

*The story of my life
is mine to share,
not yours
to invent.
I was the one living it.*

*Start burning all those bridges
so you can properly build
your own stronger foundations.
No one can do it better than you.*

*Being seen
is not the same as
being looked at.
When he, who is meant to,
Looks at you,
There won't be
Nauseating butterflies,
Or nervous energies,
Or shaking.
You will feel safe
And you will feel
loved.*

*Your blood is fluid.
Your tears are fluid.
Your energy is fluid.
Don't let your mind
be the only thing
standing in the way
towards your healing.*

*I've never known
I was cold
until I touched
warmth.*

*Blood doesn't make you
worthy,
it doesn't make you
my utmost priority
and it doesn't make me
your possession.*

*You can't see the magic
because you fear it.
You fear its power
You fear losing control.
But that's what magic
teaches you;
To lose control
into the flow
of your own
Natural Power.*

*When you stop identifying
with fear,
that's when
your true Self
will come out
into the Light.*

*You never know how deep
your love for someone is
until you need to
teach yourself
to live without them.*

*Your old ways
will never open
new doors of opportunity.
Leave the old behind;
Embrace your New You.*

Which is witch,
But witch is not
A Sinner.
For which is holy
in your truth
Is my killer.
  - Riddle

*Feeling was frowned upon
For it looked weak.
But once you free yourself,
From their old patterns,
You make the rules.*

Never fit in.
Please, never try to fit in,
For no two people are alike
And no one is actually
Just like you.

Anger, Frustration, Rage are just
Different masks for
Fear.
So what do you
Actually fear?
Learn to name
your own Demons.
- Shadow Work

*You cannot stitch a broken heart
back the same way
it was.
For it grew much bigger
than the cage it once
lived in.*

*My sickness
cannot be healed
By your unholy
thoughts.
I started peeling away
all the layers you once
covered me in.
All that breaking made
more space for Truth.*

I was ashamed of what you
Did to me.
But you said I deserved it.
And I believed you.
I saw myself weak.
I saw myself stuck
At that time...
Little did I know,
I, myself, would later be
burning your soul
out of my own
One lit candle at a time.
That's how much power
rested inside of me,
dormant for so many years.
Quietly waiting to emerge
from past lifetimes.
- Becoming a witch

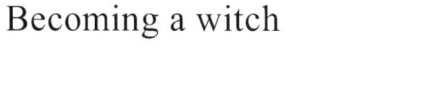

*I am the storm.
I am the wild storm that
shakes you to your core.
The wild storm that awakens
the depths of your soul.
The maddening storm that changes
who you think you are
into who you are meant to be.
No masks are allowed,
they will all be blown away
at the sight of me.*

Of love and of fate
The Gates of Hell shake.
My darling you are
All that's at stake.
Shivering vibes
Of magic and power
Awaken within you
In the midnight hour.
- Chant to awaken

*You gave me your space
I made it my home;
no one could have healed me
better than Myself.
All the breaking I did
Within myself
made more space
for whom I'm meant to be
to come alive.*

*The decaying
of my old self
is the price I must pay
for my rebirth.*

*When you're constantly battling against
the waves
At one point
your body will be so exhausted
that it shuts down.
And that's when you either drown
or allow yourself to float
and be carried to shore.
In the waves that life brought
my way,
I almost drowned.*
- Confessions

*When the sun rises
you're not looking to the West,
are you?
You're looking to the beauty
that arises from the East,
the miracle of a brand new day.
So why are you spending
so much time
dwelling on the past
When a brand new future
is arising with
each New Day that comes.*

The whispers on leaves
They vibrate through trees
The truth I do hold
Of secrets untold.
A silence so loud
That floats on a cloud
Of mist and of might
The silence is bright.
But what do I see?
The whisper is me.
I vibrate so loud
On leaves and on clouds.
I shatter and break
The truth that I take,
I come forth alive
In silence I thrive...
Speak softly to me
Of secrets and trees,
The nature is wild
I come as a child.
Blink twice and it's gone
The silence alone;
Forever alive
I come forth and dive.
   - Inner Chant

Gratitude

Florin Opris & Ioana Opris – Bancescu
- For making me feel seen & graceful
(photo credits: @Florin.Op)

Tyla Lees
- For being my second pair of eyes through this whole new Journey

Monika Cieplak Choi
- For the constant encouragement to assemble all those feelings into words.

Manufactured by Amazon.ca
Bolton, ON